Apologetic for Joy

JESSICA HIEMSTRA-VAN DER HORST

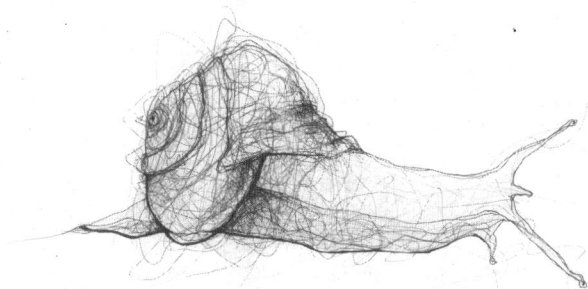

GOOSE LANE

Edited by Vanessa Moeller.
Illustrations by Jessica Hiemstra-van der Horst.
Cover and page design by Julie Scriver.
Printed in Canada.
10 9 8 7 6 5 4 3 2 1

Library and Archives Canada Cataloguing in Publication

Hiemstra-van der Horst, Jessica, 1979-
Apologetic for joy / Jessica Hiemstra-van der Horst.

Poems.
ISBN 978-0-86492-631-9

I. Title.

PS8615.I363A66 2010   C811'.6   C2010-906094-6

Goose Lane Editions acknowledges the financial support of the Canada Council for the Arts, the Government of Canada through the Canada Book Fund (CBF), and the government of New Brunswick through the Department of Wellness, Culture and Sport.

Goose Lane Editions
Suite 330, 500 Beaverbrook Court
Fredericton, New Brunswick
CANADA E3B 5X4
www.gooselane.com

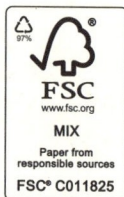

FSC
www.fsc.org
MIX
Paper from
responsible sources
FSC® C011825

Contents

Anatomy for the Artist

Eating Quince with Musicians

Bad Things Erased by Oranges

Notes for a Dying Amaryllis

Lists for the Small Brown Bat in my Heart

Slum Kidneys and Other Domestic Runaways

Confessions

For Greg—a fraction of the words I mean to say.

It begins with a mole on a white back —
a blemish of infinite potential.

Anatomy for the Artist

Anatomy for the Artist (Standing Posture, Study I)

This book, a cupboard of bones, frames
standing absurdly at attention. Pressed
between the pages of the *First Hungarian Edition*
I found two wings and antennae. Unanimated
it's not a moth.

When was the first time I ate an artichoke?

The neck, the mouth — *A* and *B,* say nothing
about the jaw going slack, an orange
rolling across the floor, the way you peeled
that artichoke, me, starting with my mouth.
Afterward, the friction of your feet,
a small cough, fragments of artichoke
like prawn tailings,

what's left when the body's consumed.

The starting point of any description of human anatomy

is the standing posture. Hooker at a bus stop.
My mother sautéing onions. Gerald in line
waiting for cabbage rolls.

You're in the shower with your eyes closed,
I'm at Food Basics visualizing your hips.
We're all in line: you in your hypothetical rain,
Gerald waiting for God, my mother stirring, erasing
her fragile ache. We're geese honking,
anticipating flight. The first stroke

determines the entire composition. This is why
an empty canvas, the future, is dangerous.
What is determined at conception, in that moment
when my father faced the wall, my mother
stood up to straighten the sheets.

Yes, Love

When you're asleep, I dream
a diagram, *a* and *b* and *c*.

a — one hair that's too long, a stray, an eyelash
on a white page, a curved note
saying something about you
can always be lost;

and *b* — your foot casually walking to nowhere
under the covers, brushing in the dark. The sound
of sheets and then on the other side of the window
a gust of wind, your shirt on the clothesline
the illusion of you;

c — how it is, how it is to sleep in the curves
of you, the hollows of a person, small miracles
that we have so many depressions, places
for each other and shadow. The arch of your foot
a road home.

This diagram is the way your body
points to mine, how we mark each other
without leaving prints. If —

if you leave, I'd be the outline
of an unhung painting, my shape
your silhouette. I'd be nothing
but a place where there used to be
the Rouen Cathedral, full sunlight.

Anatomy for the Artist (Motion, Study II)

Which muscle hauls us out of bed, contracts
when paddle hits water, draws hand
to heart in the dip and spill of grief, turns a cheek
from someone else's suffering, a fish bone
in the throat?

We step over the man asleep on the grate. Eventually
we talk about how to give, what to give. I want to
say: *let's leave this place, talk about Colville's light,*
pretty fish —

Fingertips Are for Touching

Do I leave a mark on you
when I graze by your chair?
Children understand loneliness:
they sit in laps, cry
until they are empty.

Every mark I make
on you, on canvas,
is a brush with infinity, hoping
two of us under covers
see each other without light.

Anatomy for the Artist (Light, Study III)

Fresh paint can only be touched by air
and light, shadow. That's how we should
touch, without consuming. I can't believe
I told you *I want to own you.* I meant to say
I need to watch you bend, listen to your feet
on the cold floor, fine hairs
dragged across the blue.

Falling in Love at the Lindsay Aquatorium

Bobbing in the pool, I loved his big white belly,
learned that love is a beached whale, ripples.
I loved his red trunks, their blue stripe,
that dirty nylon drawstring, always in a knot,
undoing it with his teeth on the school bus.

I can smell him still, hay bales,
before dipping in chlorine,
mentioning cows, alfalfa
and his mom.

I ache Renoir, the poem of his wrist

strapped to the brush, a parched hand
tied to his heart. In 1954 an artist died:
Matisse, who didn't get mired down in politics,
arranged armchairs in paintings, arranged
women, missed operation *Bravo*. At last,
when his body betrayed him, he kept making
collages, paradises out of furniture. I wonder —

what is it about the shuffling of the wrist,
cracks in canvas? When I'm old
will I be unafraid? Will I still
line up tomatoes on the sill, arrange
lines to make sense of debris?

Georgia's Recipes Somehow

I bought *Georgia's Kitchen* and hid it in my cupboard,
embarrassed. $14.95 to see her apron, pantry door.
My mother's friend loves *Tintin* —
embarrassed to be seen with him in public,
he carries him home under his jacket, reads him privately
with a plate of crackers. Greg teases me,
asks when I'll buy *Picasso's Guide to Auto Mechanics*.

All I want is a peek at her cupboards,
at Georgia's asparagus. I want to imagine
her hands shaving carrots, pressing garlic, husking.
I hope for secret scrawl in the margins, a recipe
for that thin union of sand and sky. I want a glimpse
of her, stooped over her garden. Peeling the plastic,
making the first bend of the spine, I see
pots on a white wall. They are Georgia's bones, her hands

buried now. Do you think someday I will excavate
her from the desert and hold her up to the sky? Remember
how often she's given us new ways to look at the moon
through a hole in an old bone. She gave me the recipe
for savouring blue, some way to capture the arc of bird,
its turn of wing, the silence of an empty skull, somehow
the pulse of desert.

Georgia's Pelvis III and IV

Georgia sees the world through an empty pelvis.
I'm holding my thumb up to my own landscape
trying to get a sense of scale. She's right: scale
is what you look through, how close to the dirt
you're willing to put your chin, how much moon
is visible peering through the dry bones
of some desert animal.

The desert is here — in Georgia's pelvises, the contrast
of blue and empty, fragments held up to sky. The moon
is a hole in an old body, a New Mexican breeze,
the memory of small feet traipsing over sand.

Looking through a hole in the barn I saw blue,
Georgia's pelvis, found a way that made sense
to frame the world, sky.

Georgia's Light, Blues

Georgia takes me someplace I've never been—
so familiar it's more like the world I know
than the one I'm in, where red has hum,
and blue's a low cello in the gut.
I'd like to touch your painted canvas,
your Jesus-robes, Georgia. Yeah—

I have this odd problem though: moths
keep sailing into my paintings, not the naked bulb,
deep in the basement. Have I made
that much light? I fly into your paintings
like that, looking for light, crash-landing
in your blue, just to touch your sunrise,
that coin of light.

I've got this sow thistle on canvas
in the basement. One moth, wings first
in the sky, died before I could save it, ruined
by a trick of light. I've attempted its excavation
but all I could do was tug body from wing.
Georgia, I think I left my wings
in your New Mexican sky.

Georgia, I'm Sorry You're Dead

I wanted to thank you
for the blue especially,
for what New Mexico did to you, for saying
the small things take time. It's you
who flicked on the lights, made this place
inexplicably luminous, light under the door
erasing the room. For not saying—

How to Finish a Painting (Final Study, IV)

End with almost,

with dark blue and ginger tea, a phone call
to your mother, however impossible,
whisper something so inaudibly
even you can't hear. Finish with your signature
silently in the corner

so that later, when you have forgotten
who you are, when you are dying,
when someone brings the painting to your bed,
you are almost

willing to believe in heaven. You can
look at your name, remember
what you wanted, something
beautiful, something—

Eating Quince with Musicians

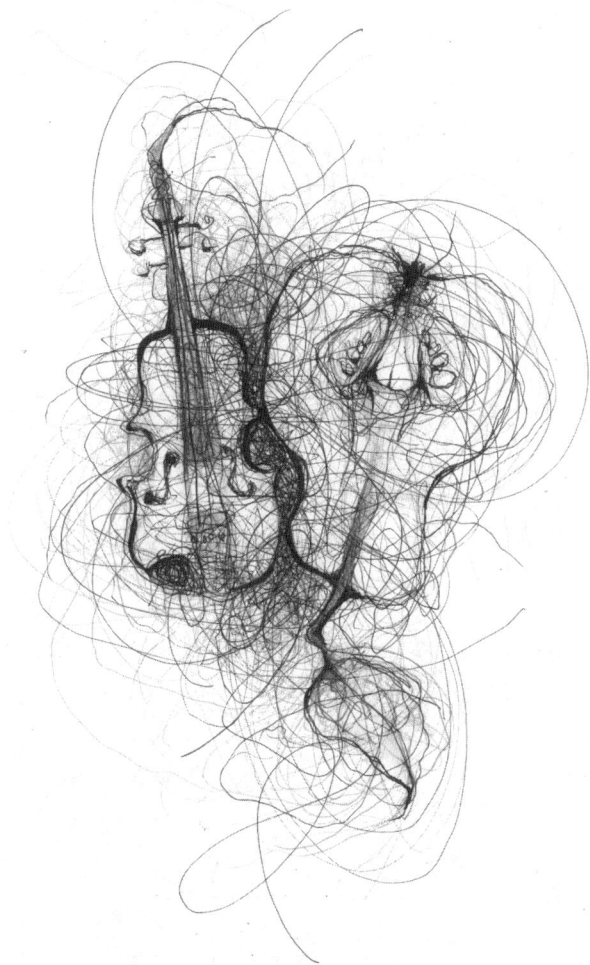

Eating Quince with Musicians

i.

I ate quince with musicians and contemplated
transformation. Deborah explained the quince:
It begins hard and yellow, she said, *needs peeling
and long heat.* Finally it is ambrosia, soft and red.
At dinner Sarah, the cellist, was saying something
that mattered, something about Van Diemen's land.
Hell in paradise, she said and urged us to visit
but it was her hands that spoke to me —
short nails, muscled along the lesser phalanges.
God, I thought, those hands could convert the granite
heart. The cellist finds us in the low notes,
and you darling, have a way —

ii.

Through dinner I watched the string players' fingers,
wrapped around wineglasses, flattening
the white tablecloth. *You transform ink into sound*,
I wanted to say, *for me* — but they knew already
so I was quiet. The quince came as no surprise to them,
though they were delighted by its perfection. Musicians
are familiar with the miracle of renovating the heart. *You should
write a poem about this*, Deborah said, *the fruit*. And I
imagined the bow in her hand, hard and taut, dragging it
across a violin. *The quince*, she said, *has come back in style*.
And you, when I think I've tired of love, pull the bay leaf out
from under your sectioned quince in cream, a rose quarter.
You wipe your hand on the embroidered cloth
and I imagine it on my back, a secret note,
the alchemy of softening stone.

iii.

The next day one quince floats in lemon water,
the one that didn't fit in the white dish, all of us
discussing Tom Waits. *He's brilliant*, you say
and the hard fruit says nothing. I'm adrift
again, remembering the boy I fell in love with
at the Lindsay pool. Roundness, I think, I was smitten
with buoyancy. I longed for the space around him,
the wake of love in water. Yes — the sheets
in disarray, the imprint of you that lasts until
I straighten the duvet, flat grass where the deer
spent the night; proof of your existence
and mine.

iv.

Tom Waits doesn't need to convince us
of his worth. His rusty voice alone in a room
is a necessity and you, a substance that carries me
and all my unnecessary sorrows. The violin lifts
an auditorium with one string. Deborah shows me
a Haiku in her cookbook, a poem that asks our hands
to our hearts. We say yes to each other. And you
draw me back with one flick of your finger
as you set the quince spinning in water, a wave
spills over the side of the crystal bowl, and love,
love displaces even me.

Bad Things Erased by Oranges

I've followed Greg to another language, and so love offers

Setswana on the side of the road. In every new country
I search for people who speak my language, art:
a door in the wall of a strange room. This is how I found
Gabosole, leaning against her house on the other side
of the world, weaving a red basket. *Teach me*, I said, *to make
baskets.* And so she offered language, names for thin strips
of palm, the needle: *mokola, lemao.* I chew her words, learn
to put *tsitsiri* in my mouth, make the palm soft enough
to use. She writes her name in my sketchbook, recaps my pen,
says her friends call her *Dorkas*, and I consider —
does it matter that her name began with gazelle in Aramaic,
that gazelle became Tabitha became Dorkas? What bearing
do our origins have? What can we gain in translation?

There is a pool of hippos, tough skinned and rump bitten

somewhere close. This morning planes elevate into the blue,
take visitors over water and grass, past giraffes
running from the shadow of a scenic flight.
I am lost on the ground, sand flung up my calves
and matted into the necks of donkeys.
Goats along the highway are knuckling up brush.
When I arrive there are chicken tracks, haphazard
beside the mat, *koko* and *kokwano*, Dorkas tells me,
chickens and *chicks*, peeping and tapping, the little ones
flee my shadow, tuck under a grey hen's wing.

Later, the day gathers into a green wall,
the shadow of one brown leaf after another falls into sand,
sand that has found its way into every corner.
Kokwano, I whisper, *which shadows am I running from?*

But *Emaha*:
stop. It's the small beauties that tug, suddenly my profile
illuminated by an old lamp, even on a dirty wall, lovely.

Bus-ring or bus-rink, we can't decide. I think it's ring

but Greg thinks it's rink so I tease him. *Picture buses*
on roller skates I say, *circling Maun.* Dorkas loves
Mosophane, whose last name means *bad things.*
What does it mean when he brings me an orange?
I haven't asked the word for dog yet. I see them
everywhere, all bone and pelvis, eaten from the inside
by smaller carnivores. Everything is hungry, even me
eating an orange while they rummage through peels
and chicken bones. And then I see one, bus-hit
at the bus-ring or bus-rink. It cries in a way that convinces me
but I acknowledge it only by my blink, my intention
to bring hand to heart. I am eating so I do nothing
but toss the peel, continue. *Dilodibe:* bad things,
erased by oranges.

I'm even a stranger to the shadows on the wall, leaves

from a tree I can't name, a substance hidden in language
only beginning to unfurl. *Ke bata go ithuta,* Gabosale says to me,
one hand over her heart. *Ke bata go ithuta Setswana.* The wall
is leaves shimmering, vocabulary I'll never learn. Beauty
is like that, isn't it? No word for the sparrow movement
of Gabosale's hands as she weaves her basket, no word
for the ache in the chest caused by silhouettes. There is
no phrase to convey the pleasant discomfort of being
foreigner, a strange shadow on an old wall. *Ke bata, ke bata —*
I want, I want to recognize the shadows, the flicker
of leaves that have names. I want to ask for an orange
in Setswana. *Ke bata go ithuta:* I want to learn,
to weave substance with shadow.

We were both wrong, or maybe it's a spelling mistake

Bus rank, we find out, and examine the brochure
closely, ask ourselves, *is one bus better than another?*
Is there some order to the way they line up, doors open,
skirts, orange peels and boxes spill out? What you think
you hear changes everything. But *go siame*:
it's all right, another way to say goodbye.

Yesterday I learned the tree outside is dying

each leaf falls because of a small white worm.
And Mosophane tells me about the dog
stretched in the sand against their house.
It was hit, he says, *by one car and then another.*
He feeds it, says it's getting better
although every time it eats, it throws up. Perhaps
it's the same white worm gorging my tree. *Iwala*,
he says, sick. And I ask him in my new language:
O tsogile jang — how did you rise this morning?
Ke a Iwala, he says, I am sick. Something is wrong
with his stomach and I want the word
for eating from the inside.

Motse: home. **Gabosale tells me**

the chicks belong to the neighbour
but they choose to live here. Animals
don't discern property lines. I tell her
my neighbour shot our dog
because it visited too many times. *But,*
she says, *lefatshe:* this world,
it is not mine.

A year later a small voice on the other line. It's Dorkas

her voice thin and strange in my ear. My basket,
half-finished, is on the kitchen counter. Our friendship,
half-started, is divided by ocean and distance. Somewhere
between us, I think, someone is eating an orange. *My husband*
she says, *Mosophane is dead. Oh Dorkas*, I say, *are you all right?*
Language is inadequate, I say, and she doesn't understand.
I'm fine, she tells me, and our connection is lost.
                                                    Gabosale
Morokotso, *Morokotso*, the last little bit of milk left in a teat.
I see Mosophane on a steel bucket demonstrating
in quick gestures the tug and squeeze of milking
an imaginary udder on an imaginary cow. I close my eyes
to see his small white shorts, running shoes, oranges.
His last words to me, *tsamaya sentle*: go well.
How did he leave? But I can't ask when I call back
and so I say what I can. *Ke a go rata,* I say again, again,
Ke a go rata: I love you, by now the only Setswana
I can remember. *I bought an orange today*, I say.

Notes for a Dying Amaryllis

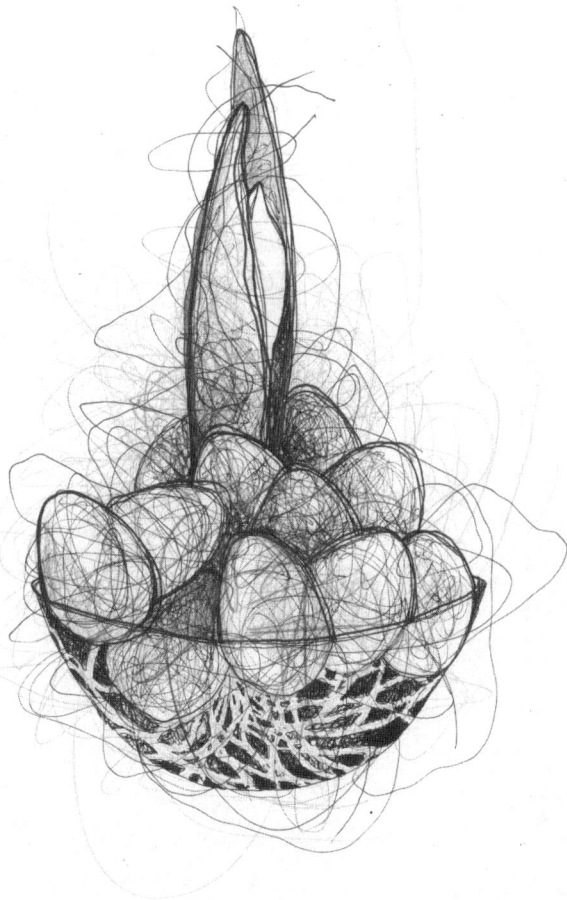

Note Left in a Dash on the Studio Fridge

Amaryllis—

tell me again how to mix light
to make green
that you and I need sunlight
like water,
both of us places
for the sun to pool.

On your lips, the secret we've unearthed
staring into each other all morning:
beauty is neither rare nor fragile—

abundant green fists on the lilac out the window,
Oma's red toenails, the dog's head cocked, listening
to the goose leaving water, a smooth white canvas
unrippled, so far—

My World Is Still Flat

I don't want my world to spin. God painted
on a sphere, an unfolding installation
that cuts faith loose. I'm not Job —
the last earthquake swallowed my confidence.

Entropy is too much for me, spinning
my brush in red paint. I can't work
with a palette of infinity and suffering
and still find redemption. I can cope
with only one moment of chaos
or ecstasy. On our sheets
I grasp the world, on canvas
make a dying amaryllis matter.

When I Go to Heaven I'm Going to Miss Avocados

A small detail, but they taste too much like earth
to be in paradise. Okay then, no avocados,
but what about my Strawberry Shortcake sneakers?
Buried when I was ten, carcasses under rubbish
at the municipal dump. Quick—

before I lounge on greener pastures
I'll dash to the beach in white ankles
and a ridiculous sunhat, eat an avocado
in my skinnies. Does paradise have room enough
for Strawberry Shortcake sneakers, shadows
of telephone wires on snow, lulls in traffic, bad reception
on the radio? Where will all the dilapidated houses go,
along with their beautiful sorrows? I'm going to miss cussing
and pleading with a God who never answers.
Will there be a little hole to peek through
at the bottom of heaven? I'm not ready to give up
lying on my back, deciphering clouds.

The Substance of Almost

Gerald's been complaining about a mouse in the wall.
For weeks I've assumed it's in his head. Everything we see
is mixed with three colours and shades of darkness.
The mouse is almost real, I'm almost content, this flower
on canvas—not quite. We need something else, someone else
to prove that we're here, to confirm the mouse
scratching in the dark.

I want to find the world in dust on a tabletop,
the motion of a petal falling, the turn of a cheek
after laughing.

Prescriptions for Katherine (not your real name)

It starts with your name, the violence of not using it,
not naming you or how you've been treated
like a horse or a suitcase. You fell. Lost luggage,
lame thoroughbred. A doctor with a clipboard
picked you up by the armpits, scribbled your fate
in other names: *Bupropion, Celexa*. He handed you
a slip that says *come back next month*.
Under fluorescent lights you can say
my unhappiness is debilitating. I don't know

your anatomy well enough, only how your skin
folds into your armpit, how you come into focus
when you smile. I'd like to prescribe disobedience,
a ride around the baggage claim at terminal three,
petting a horse, exhaling into its nostrils.

How to Cut a Chicken into Little Pieces

The yellow tablets cause momentary blindness,
keep Gerald standing straight up dizzy. It's better
for him to be thirsty than dead, it's better
for him to stop making love, to be
sedate. Because at least parched I can take him
on the bus, visit his friend Lydia at the church
who shows him how to make chicken and rice,
ignores his sudden Polish and God, demonstrates
with a dead hen —

snip the fat here, she says, *pull the wings from the body,*
cut between the cartilage, separate the breasts
from the ribs. He lays all the pieces neatly
on a bed of rice. But first she holds the bird
over the gas flame, singes the stubs of feathers.
No one wants to see feathers, she says.
That part of the bird reminds us of flying.

To be or not to be, says Gerald, *that is the question.*
Lydia puts her scissors on the counter and Gerald
recites the whole thing without inflection. *They jumped,*
he says, on the heels of *all my sins remembered. I think,*
he says, *she thought she could fly.* Lydia doesn't know
about Gerald's Ophelia or his father. *They're dead,*
he says, *that simple.*

Getting Out of the House
(for DF)

Your inability to admit entropy makes you sit
all afternoon in the same chair, sun up sun down
go to bed. The ketchup is going to fall over, lint
will gather at the elbows. Things spill, arrive late.
Hair curls into the corners of the kitchen, people chew
with their mouths open, uninvited mice run across
the counter, lick the faucet when no one's looking.

I don't presume to understand, but the day the sidewalk
tripped you, your coffee spilled down your shirt.
Your knee bloomed red and your universe,
so carefully constructed, was suddenly a black hole.
A rip in your jeans. You unravelled. It became dangerous
to get coffee. You tell me, *I used to swim,*
lick icing out of the bowl.

Excerpts from Gerald, God and the Chickens

ii

Looking for God in unlikely places, we found him
buried in the bottom of a box of frozen chicken strips.

I think he was hiding, a little concerned about the death of the pope,
a little troubled by the disappearance of fairies.
Gerald says God would like to nick a wand or a potion,
pretend he's Luke Skywalker for a day. People are lost
without figures with staffs or wands. And God's got nothing
to hold in his hand to shake or wiggle to change the world.
I guess that's why he was in the chicken. He needed some quiet,
some time to think about the pope and why people get schizophrenia
or why we've blamed him for suffering. I think he was reflecting
on translation — what's become of the women and the chickens.
He looked as if he hadn't slept in years. So we held him awhile,
myself and Gerald, who whispered in Polish
that it wasn't God's fault, that he should come out of the chicken,
maybe tell us a joke. Gerald says the world's okay like this;
there are a few things that could be different,
but the chickens and the women were a good idea.

ix

We found him in front of the monitor,
googling the pope, wondering how he got involved
in debates over condoms. God sits at the computer, chin in hand,
touches the screen with the finger he used to point with.
This is an unusual alliance, he tells Gerald, adrift in Wikipedia,
reading about crosiers and excommunication.
He confides in Gerald that he'd hoped
we'd take life a little more intuitively.
He hasn't spoken in a very long time
and now he's worried that anything he says will be
taken too seriously.

v

We found God slumped on the veranda,
a rose in his teeth and a thin woman on his lap
trying to get his attention, praying fiercely
into his ear. Rocking back and forth,
God said something about proximity,
something about the rose and the thorn.
Between me and you, he said,
the difference between heaven and hell
is distance. Gerald kneeled, whispered to him
about paradise, about grabbing a coffee.

vii

We caught him trying to use the force,
sitting on the curb, hands stuffed in his blue coat pockets.
He was trying to put the recycling away just by looking.
Gerald hauled the bin to the garage.

I've lost my concentration, God tells Gerald,
if had a light sabre I might find my way in the dark,
restore the world with a flick of the wrist.
Gerald tells God it's just a story.
I know, God moans, *but I can't help believing.*

viii

We lost God again. We found him wandering,
dishevelled in his blue pyjamas, shifting
from foot to foot in Food Basics, holding a jar
of light green artichoke hearts. Gerald says
God comes here when he needs order:
rows of cans and freezers, straight lines.

God says he's lost. He's been watching the news again,
thinking about birds that can't fly.
He comes here for something else to gnaw on:
the idea of tuna packed in little red cans,
vacuum-packed chicken patties, neatly sealed packages
of beef liver, lean strips for stirfry.

God says death this small is easier to grasp.

xii

Gerald decided it was time God learned stick shift.
He says if God had a little more control, a little less
automatic, he might feel like he's in charge again.
God drives like Gerald's *dziadek*, distracted
by the noise of wipers, startled
by stoplights and signs. God, in the driver's seat,
can't help lingering around the ankles
of finely-crafted women. *This isn't lecherous
old man stuff*, he tells Gerald. He says
to look longer at limbs, the quiet angle
of a branch over a bridge, an arm hooked around a waist.
In a soft voice, he confides, *I have nothing left to say
about the difference between right and wrong, the distance
between me and you. But sorrow and beauty, hand and heart,
love and pity —*

*the naked arch of a deer stopped forever,
curved on the side of the highway —*

Try to decipher that, he says.

xxi

At 10 they watch the news,
sock feet on the coffee table.

God's distressed, says Gerald, about divorce.
Not the one between husbands and wives
(people get tired, love gets tired),
but the one between green and rest, fact
and fiction, men and children. He's sick of us
translating dichotomy into his poems
and he's been trying to make sense of purgatory.

He turns to Gerald on the other end of the couch,
It seems, he says, *they think they suffer for a reason.*

xxvii

We find God cross-legged on the kitchen floor
with a box of frozen wings in his lap.
So many wings and no birds, he says
and plunges a hand into the box.
I'm up to the elbow in wing knuckles, he tells Gerald,
and I've counted an odd number —
one bird had only one wing, he says,
and what have they done with the bodies?
These wings have nothing to carry.

He lifts his old hand out of the box.
It's not right, he says. *Wings make sense in motion,*
earth makes sense in motion. When we stop spinning
sorrow finds a place to settle.
Gerald squeezes God's hand. *So cold,*
he says, *let me blow on your fingers.*
God withdraws his other hand and offers it to Gerald.
What's the point of a creature who can't fly, he says.
Icarus, says Gerald, and leaves it at that.

xxiii

God says he's changed, an old man now
and contemplating paradise, the blue veins in his hands.
He looks up and gets lost in the arc of a seagull. *Wings*, he says,
are marvellous, the universe is held together by flight.

But he's perplexed by the chicken —
flightless and silly. *One could argue*, he tells Gerald,
chickens are more useful dead
than alive. If this is the case, he says,
the universe will unravel.

xxxiii

I've made a tray of sandwiches. Toothpick umbrellas
in crunchy peanut butter and raspberry.
Gerald shuffles into the kitchen in plaid pyjamas,
his favourite red Ferrari shirt, and asks for a peanut butter and jam.
God slides him the platter, asks if he'd like anything else.

Heal me from schizophrenia, says Gerald,
and God snaps his fingers. Gerald raises his hands in the air,
elbows out like a startled hen. *I'm healed*,
he laughs, and takes a bite. *Saving*, says God,
is a complicated business. I wish
there was a way. Gerald pulls the umbrella out of his sandwich
and offers God a bite of his peanut butter and jam.
But God declines——*I'm not hungry for jam*, he says.
You have to eat, says Gerald, *despite the news.*

xxxviii

Usually God slips in through the window,
but this Sunday he tells Gerald he's weary of church.
The hymns are lovely, he says, *but I'm tired
of sermons, crusades.* Preludes and sunlight
don't lift him anymore. He has a postcard of St. Peter's Pietà
pinned to his headboard. *It's only the memory of love*, he says,
*there's nothing left to believe. Isaiah made promises
I couldn't keep, prayer's reduced to words.*

Gerald takes God's hands. *My hands*, says Gerald,
are folded in surrender, not prayer.

lii

God brings a chicken up from the basement,
vacuum-packed and headless.
Gerald opens the door for God.
Their bodies persist, says Gerald,
without their minds.

God lifts the bird into the roaster.
Tell me then, he says, *what's the point
of the chicken?*

Gerald looks God in the eye.
*Chickens sleep without concern
and panic without guilt.
They die without regret
and run without grace. Chickens
are surprised by the world every day —
and they only fly by accident.*

Lists for the Small Brown Bat in my Heart

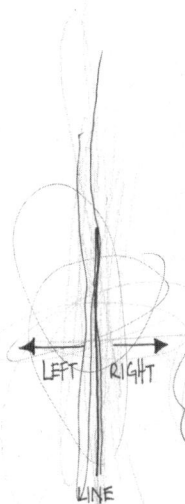

LINE

LEFT ←→ RIGHT

Simle direction.
Splits space into 2.

OUT ↑
IN ↓

CIRCLE

Same in all directions.
Splits space into inside
& outside.

SPIRAL

Directional variability.
Inside and outside connection.

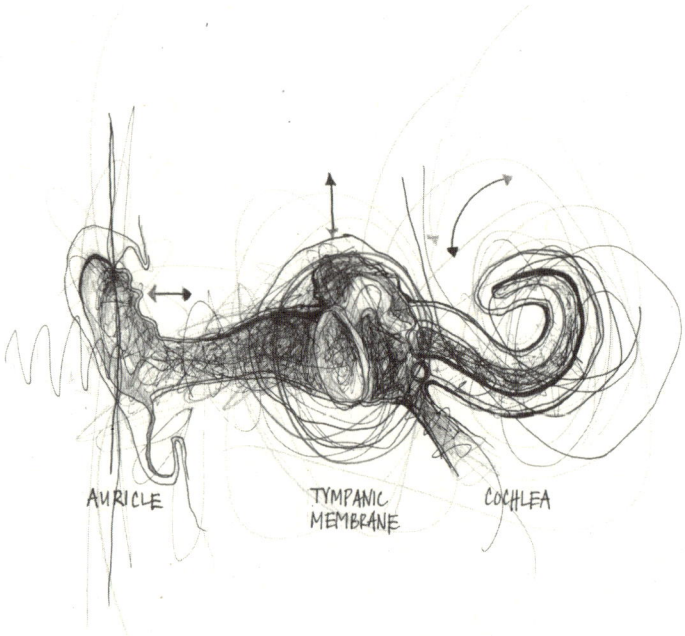

AURICLE   TYMPANIC   COCHLEA
MEMBRANE

The magpies in Melbourne have bells in their chests

First day, 5 a.m., church bells on the windowsill, the sway
of eucalyptus in the dark. I reached over to find you
in my bed, awake, smelling of oranges and sleep.
Learning this new country is falling in love. I'm enamoured
with unannounced callas in the corners of every yard,
succulents and lavender, sage
in unexpected places.

The magpie shakes her bells and you
shake awake. I recall the discovery of you,
the first time I fell asleep in your neck,
that sweet unexpected plot.

What did I bring from the old country? Another way

to say *basil, tomato*, a useless cord for a hair blower
that can't hold the voltage. We run on arbitrary amounts
of power — 120, 240, one cup of coffee. The mistake
is thinking we speak the same language: lovers
and the English continents. But if we stop fussing with words
we find each other in new ways. Deborah and I this morning
bent at the nasturtium, extravagant droplets balanced
like fat hens on each leaf, Gabosale leaning against me
warm and brown, hair wedged under her red hat,
the two of us watching chickens tuck in for the night. And you,
always you, slipping my hair behind my ear in the dim
when you thought I had drifted. Learning an unknown country
is divining water in pairs, the warmth of two bodies; fuel
for the bells in our chests.

In British Columbia I took long showers, soaked

in the tub when a painting got ornery. Home,
the one I know, is water: you and my coast,
mostly rain. The drought here has lasted 10 years.
Trucks cruise the highway with water tanks,
yellow ratchet straps. There must have been
a blue pail sale: shower stalls are equipped with cobalt
and a red handle to irrigate limes, new potatoes.
I try to rinse without wasting but it's impossible,
isn't it? I tell you I love you when you're not here
and yesterday you dragged me out of the house
to show me the sky. *Look*, you said, and I didn't
care enough, which meant my love was inadequate.
I want the excessiveness of love without catchment—
where do all the words we mean to say go?

I migrate to the teakettle, the window — in search

of errant red leaves. At night, feet on cool tile,
I bump the fridge, open it, white light. I find
my way by the noise of the objects around me. You
snoring lightly, the hum of the fridge, a faucet
that needs a washer. Small brown bats find their way
by singing past obstacles. Wind turbines are detonating
their lungs. Their chests expand before they are able
to exhale. I remember explosive fullness, my oboe
and Sunday dress in front of church, 12 years old
and 12 bars in, my nervous habit of inhaling when afraid.
I tried to squeeze it out through music, one small reed.

Are bats uneasy as they approach the blades
or do they just sing and collapse?

There are rabbits here, imported foxes,
feral camels. We think we can fix our planet
by adding to it. Georgia's cookbook had us giggling:
the recipe for spinach: *add water, steam*.

Simplicity confounds us,
sets us in spiral.

This morning the tub was full of cold water

9-year-old Isabella's goggles, a loose ribbon
like a leaf underwater. When do we stop playing
our way through ordinary moments? Yesterday Kurt
asked: *any joy today?* I pulled the nasturtiums
out of the soil, planted potatoes. *God*, I didn't say,
I take pleasure in work. I've become protestant
to endure chores. There are two kinds of joy:
the joy we grow into and the joy we grow out of.
I remember my mother telling me: *if you hang your shirts*
you'll be happy later. I was baffled but now I realize
pegging your blue-striped button-up, my old bra,
I look forward to folding, tucking into drawers.
In the garden there are secret potatoes that will sprout.
They've begun their search for sun and water and so
I find joy in dappled light on laundry, waiting
for potatoes — the fringes where pleasure
meets utility. But I should have refilled the tub,
donned Isabella's gear, searched the enamel basin
for crayfish, treasure, rediscovered what it's like
to find an ocean in a bucket.

Clyde the cat has started a course of antibiotics

Deborah and Kurt knew he was sick because he was
afraid, skittish, because he was looking for a quiet angle
to conclude in. The first time I cut into a blood orange
I was startled to find death nestled in beauty.
Every object has the hue of its fate hidden in it —
before Dad abandoned us he was grey, the future
had already drawn the colour from him
and he took to scouring the dishes, as if that might
wash the future. Mosophane sat on a pail and scrubbed
leftover pasta from an aluminum pan. *I'm tired*
he said, *so tired*. But just when I think this poem
is about death, it's about medicine. Isabella and Annika
showed me their wrists this morning: *ballerinas hold
their hands like so* they said and demonstrated
their *pas de chats*. As Clyde recovers, he eyes me
at the sink, rinsing and loving my father, a new
country. And you, flush with desire, wait
for me under a duvet, the future written
on your lips, mine.

I continue to look for God, and I wonder

i.

if God's searching for me too. Plato imagined souls drifting
in the sphere of ideas, undone halves waiting to be made
whole. I don't know what I believe. I am certain of you,
drawn home to me on your bicycle. I am homesick and wistful
of cedar, but all my desire cannot tug a continent, no matter
the claims of the lovelorn. What I miss is recognition: a kitchen
I've scoured over and over, cupboards slammed in red moments,
opened in search of coconut milk, small appetites, answers
to prayer. I miss trees whose sway I trust with windows closed,
eyes shut. I know what I want is approximate: it is the trace
of a landscape transposed by the heart. It is the echo of my feet
in Green Timbers Park, one stone knocking another
on Jericho Beach, having sought each other since Pangaea
fragmented, just to make one soft note. Home knows us
because it becomes us, because we breathe it day after day
until we are composed
of what it casts. And so —

ii.

How can I paint what I do not know? I want the blue rim
of Texada, skytrain, dark grey of a polished otter, slow rain.
I don't know how to ask God here because the birds are
dazzling and unknown. In my own country I know the curves
of my lexicon, the indignant burst of crow. I can imagine God
crouched on shore when the salmon fatigue. The stones
at St. Kilda's have found each other so often they have become
sand, tapping so quietly only jellyfish hear. I sit in an empty room
waiting for you, for God. My room is bare, a pair of red curtains
and I am a matador flicking them open, conscious of you pedalling
to me, propelling yourself in my direction. Is God
the wrists of Isabella, an address, the smooth fit of you and me
in the night? Is the jellyfish, slowly coasting toward its necessity,
searching or being found? Is home learning to be persuaded
by eucalyptus, aram lilies? I'd like to think I can be completed,
that home will find me if I wait with my only flag — drawing
and withdrawing curtains in a silent room, semaphoring
my desire to be made whole, answered by the divine, you.

The universe divides and divides. When I dream

of the primordial stew, I see our skating rink in summer,
marsh marigolds and methane, the occasional remains
of a lost cow buried and forgotten. Georgia saw the cosmos
in old bones, the constellation of us halved and halved. Life
is a riddle: we are made by being broken
and I can pour the dead body of a carp on my lavender
so the impulse of a murky fish renders ultraviolet. Vivaldi,
long dead, continues to play through hands of new
musicians, old strings. This morning in the bookstore,
skimming the poetry section for familiar notes, I grew
even farther from my mother because I could hear her
humming *Four Seasons* in the herb garden. I began
in the empty sky of her, a mauve seed that bloomed
and bloomed. At first transparent, I grew fingers and toes,
dendrites so I could learn to reach. I became substance; divided
until I was whole. But now the Southern Cross winks
in my sky and Polaris in hers. We are divided
by continents, waypoints for different constellations
and I'm not sure which theory I ascribe to: some say
the universe is expanding, others that it is collapsing.
I wonder, does my division have a trajectory —
am I drawn to my mother, or from her?

Pleasure is always unexpected, soft green

i.

of a new pea about to break the surface, my nephew,
eyes closed underwater, having his hair rinsed,
attuned to the glide of his own body under the water.
We are whales; we are catalysts and substance, the dust
of all the bones and detritus of time. I have an affinity
for lavender because it was once part of me, because
we began in the same soup, afraid of the same sudden
light. Pleasure is orange calendula on stage this morning
when I pull back the red curtains, introduce them
to their audience: your yellow bicycle, a Toyota Camry,
the 10 o'clock Moms tucking fitness between snacks
and naps and onesies and spoons. It is you choosing
your jeans, selecting a lime for me, arranging romas,
buying a bell for your handlebars. Love is visualizing

ii.

you selecting vegetables — arbitrary and considered,
how I picked you because I wanted you, though I don't
grasp why. Do I love you because you were once
part of me and a strange umbel, because we sang together
in the Pacific, ate krill and scraped ourselves on barnacles
for pleasure? Have my cells been pining for you for eons,
lost and lonely in the skin of guava and lions and, finally,
in this body, parallel enough to sense you again? Is it you
I return to under the orange sheets, or is it a fraction of me
that went astray? I know: I have found another way to ask
the same question, that soul one. Are we what we are
or what we were? I don't need to know though I want to.
The lavender in me says *it doesn't matter*, the outcome
is the same: you come home with a lime for Thai
and I take pleasure in cutting lengthwise,
finding your skin, mine.

Homesickness is a small brown bat

in my chest writing lists, tied to a taut cord.
When I was small I lived in Badala, where we
used to unplug our attic, not of bric-a-brac
and old chests crammed with Emily Dickinson,
but of soft new bats. Our neighbours' children
fashioned kites that didn't need wind. They tied
bats to their wrists. The creatures fatigued, flailing
for liberty. This is why we hoist kites,
run until something tied to our body
is airborne.

The bats worried themselves loose, or died
trying to return home.

I get a little lost in my navel sometimes. And so

I thought I'd invite you to rescue me. I've tugged in Johnny Cash
and Susan Sontag, Yann and his menagerie. I dragged in Tracy Emin
with her bed and her rage and her clamouring to reach us, reach out
to us. I've pulled in Mary Pratt and a punnet of strawberries, orange peels
and the whirr of my hard drive and the smell of gel medium
and my parents' old chairs and the small notes of owls and August
wolves. I need you to drop your arm and pull me up, because when I try
to crawl out of the hole I was born with, I fall back in. I need you
to tell me I make art for a reason. You see, I don't need to be seen,
I want to be heard. I want to take your hand and put it under a hen's wing.
I want to say: *loveliness, look, it's here.* It's hidden in calendula, broken teeth,
the woman who told me God stops the rain for her. *I say look Lord,*
I'm tired of the rain, she told me. I feel obligated to cut a cow in half, holler
hell. I should. But every time I'm flooded, I'm flooded with splendour.
I want to paint the way I love Vancouver, the way it seeps through me,
the fling of water from spokes, the wash of winter on skytrain windows,
the underbelly of eagles, the undersides of frogs, leaves.
There's a whirlpool in my navel, the Zambezi kind, the kind that spins
you so deep you're never found. Somewhere at the bottom of chaos
is silence, trapped horses, a man in a kayak who never emerged.

My friend Erin wrote a poem about the horse latitudes, a terrible quiet
that makes you toss your metaphors for hope into the sea. I'm ready
to fling my paintings so I can change my geography. I'm ready to burn
everything I love to budge.

        Stop me. Save me from my horse latitudes,
my spiral to the bottom of nothing. Join my mother, whisper to me. Tell me:
do what you want; it's brave to be adrift with love.

Oma rode a bicycle for four years in a room of mattresses

i.

and blankets. She took turns with her sisters, pedalling
and singing hymns to keep a flicker in the room. Imagine
learning to ride a bicycle in a dark room, going nowhere
but generating the future, light out of friction. They sang
for the dead man tied to a parachute, hope with holes in it,
the kind of failure the human heart can't figure. This is how
we find our balance: by pedalling, flying despite the impossibility
of it. Oma's father kept bees on that roof. Another beautiful thing,
the trick of keeping something that has the freedom to leave
but chooses return. I don't know what happened to the bees
during the war, if some were caught in the Hamburg updraft
while pulling nectar, while Oma and her sisters spun their feet,
watched the plume, sparks from German blankets,

ii.

burning bicycle tires. I wonder if a bee can get flung in crossfire.
I suppose so, however absurd the accident of plucking a bee
from the blue with a bullet. I don't know why they continue
to make honey while we make war. Mostly I don't know
what it means. It could be a metaphor for the necessity of love
or oblivion, but it's hard to imagine that heavy trill, wings in a field
of whimpering soldiers, flat grass. I don't have faith it means anything
except that clover finds the sun because it has to, that a bee finds a flower
because it is the only urgency it knows, that a soldier finds a pocket
for a photo: a roof for memory to land, atop the boarded up room
of longing. The heart is where we store honey and purpose. It is
a house balanced on song and a bicycle, a place for bees to touch down
and make pleasure, or whatever
it is they do.

Yesterday I listened to Oma's funeral, recorded

i.

for those of us who couldn't attend. I needed confirmation
that she had stopped thrumming. Until now I failed to believe
it was true. I was born to doubt because all the evidence
says she isn't silenced. The peas are reaching for the wall,
the smell of lavender is on my hands, trimming and tacking
this poem. Music persists, it is everywhere: Greg's spoon
skimming the rim of his Earl Grey, the one-two-one-two
of bicycling legs past my window, magpies transforming
the morning by shaking their bells. And Maya Angelou,
who they tell me won't live forever, sings this moment
though all the evidence suggests she is asleep. She tells me
the bird doesn't sing because it has an answer, it sings
because it has a song.

ii.

Maya is in my studio because I can imagine her
in a red dress, because I hear her voice in the symphony
surging from a small speaker on my laptop, the chorus
of The Silesia Philharmonic singing of the *tongues of angels*.
Maya told us about songbirds long ago, though the truth
is contradictory. She said it today, but it took this long
to reach me. Her words had to traverse her capillaries
to her complicated mouth, to the one-two-one-two
of fingers that posted it online. Songbirds trill from wires,
the circuitry of my laptop, the pole casting a shadow
on Oma's stone, the stone that says
I will sing —

Slum Kidneys and Other Domestic Runaways

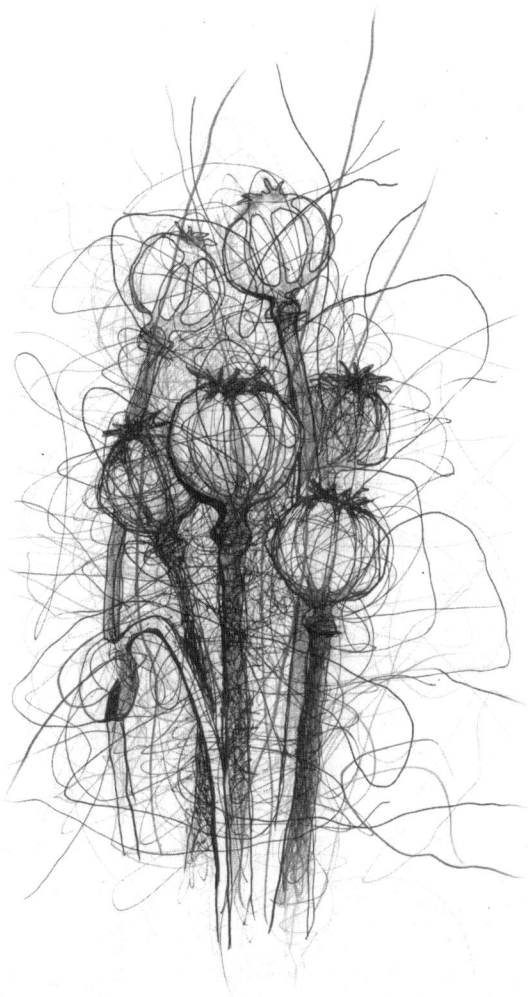

"Lost bird: tame yellow cockatiel, generous reward"

the poster said. I imagined lifting my palms
skyward with sunflower seeds, poppies, offering
my index finger as a place to land, to tempt
lemon flybys with domesticity. But the cockatiel
is Australian so it's not disoriented; it has found
an earlier perch. There are feral chickens, camels,
wild pigs. In Manoa, a pack of trained dogs
chewed the ears off a prized potbelly. *An accident,*
the authorities said, *a victim of circumstance.* We all bite
from time to time. Today on the news a murder
without backstory. Only: *the perpetrator killed*
a 14-year-old for sitting in his chair and I thought
about all of us raising our arms on occasion
for our own sweet cushion, emancipation.

"I am a 31-year-old Caucasian in perfect health

non smoker and drug free," the ad said. I was browsing
for a sofa, embroidered bedding, when I found Zack Jones
selling his kidney to the *right recipient* in 24 Ariel bold.
How much is it worth? According to the virtual world,
Western organ hunters charge as much as $85,000 for slum kidneys
from Manila. What is Zack's kidney? What makes it
a marketable appendage? Did he and his kidney
have a falling out, does it have dangerous predilections,
and how clean is Zack exactly? Does he hide ample women
under his mattress, is he addicted to the *Antique Roadshow*,
does he love perfect cups, macaroons? Has his kidney
been purifying sliced cheese and chocolate milk
since he was a boy? Is it lazy, predisposed to scratch and wins?
What makes a person decide to sell themselves? I ask Greg.
Love or poverty, he says. *Would you buy my kidney?* I ask.
No, he says, *I want everything, je veux tout
le monde entier, all of you.*

The canary tram says *"Peret created the distinctive yellow*

livery to symbolize a ray of sunlight," and hurtling
on the rails I know: no one has the reins on radiance.
Sunlight is not a yellow tram. It's not *the beeline,*
despite Peret's yearning. Light travels the tremor
of this morning's old woman pointing to the bleached
socks of lawn bowlers; it's the whisper of a moving bicycle
on a white wall; what remains of violet on the fingertips
after pinching lavender. It can't be explained by what it is
because lavender is 230 parts red, 230 green, 250 blue
and that explains nothing. Lavender is yesterday's
braided girl brushed with Oma's perfume, a Roman bath.
It's without warning being transported to Oma's glazed bowl,
spilled grapes, the radio tuned to *Requiem.* Sunlight
can't carry us on the 96 to Brunswick East, but slips
under a door, lifts us like Oma's love, Mozart. It has no mass
but the body which carries it, always returning
to the same destination: four chambers, a secret sprig
of stolen lavender in my pocket, travelling light in the dark.

Across from the tram stop, the wall says

"Therèse, I really <u>am</u> sorry." I imagine a 2 a.m. Banksy,
a penitent sinner. I'm going to scribble in the night,
request an update: *Therèse, did you forgive?* Did you find
your lover in an alley clutching a bouquet of regret,
did you believe the scrawl offered on concrete
in East Brunswick? My father burnt the maple syrup
when I was small, smoked us out with scalded sugar
and curses. He flung my mother's favourite pot into snow,
hard black mesa. She wasn't home so he proclaimed in felt tip
on our wide white Crokinole box: *n baran nyina, I'm sorry.*
My mother forgave him before she opened the door,
before the char filled her nose. She scoured the pot
with sand and water and love. This is the only grace
I know: my mother choosing to forgive my father. Agape:
love so broken open the self falls out. When he left
I searched for the Crokinole box, hoped
to make everything all right.

I'm trying to live with mice, but it's hard

I imagine them licking the breadknife, slipping into the sink
for stray bits of sourdough when I bend into the napkin drawer.
This summer Mom said she was the *interstate*, mice scrambling
over her all night long in Freetown. When I was small she knocked
on cupboards before opening, gave our cockroaches adequate time
to gather their legs and antennae, scoot out the back. *What you can't see
doesn't exist,* she told us, so I became an ostrich by inheritance.
What else did I inherit? Love for Rembrandt, desire for salt, fear
of the bubonic plague. The dog at my feet is tuned to herd cattle,
though she hasn't ever clipped a heel. And the hen withdraws
from the shadow of a hawk, though she's spent her life in sanctuary.
I am what my body remembers, the memory of my mother knocking
on cupboards. A small part of me is Oma Heerema shooing pigeons
from the attic, gathering eggs in the rim of her blouse. Instinct
is our ancestors coughing in the room of our bodies, reminding us
of falcons and heifers, the plague skittering up pipes in the ears
of rodents, the bellies of fleas. And so, I knock on drawers
before opening them. *If you're there,*
I say, *you don't exist.*

A new country is learning small creatures, the cornflowers

i.

I planted as an act of faith — in home, green. I'm learning
the eddies, the tug of my new city, new magpies. Discerning
the universe is a tricky business. Tell me, what does it mean
that my bicycle was stolen? My sweetheart teases me:
you didn't love it enough, and he's right, but I don't think love
is ever enough. I planted cornflowers because I love waiting
for their sunny blue faces, watching the complicated ease
of their exchange with sun, wind, bees. I've loved them
as much as I can, and since my bicycle was stolen I've tried
to love them more. I've watered gently, sung hymns to them.
But in the night, despite my love and desire, a slow appetite
tugs my metaphor into its long abdomen, swallows the green
lobes, my faith. The problem isn't that there are no more

ii.

bikes or cornflowers, because there are. The problem is
that nothing can be replaced with what it was. I must plant
a new seed and find a new pair of pedals and, despite tending
to them with all my love, my cornflowers fail. Love, you see,
is always inadequate. It meets accident and crows, slow burglars.
Some things, when they're gone, are gone forever. Oma
is sown under stone, and the passenger pigeon has transformed
into an allegory for a kind of gluttony that frightens me.
The marsupial tiger I've just discovered, thylacine, has come
and gone, replaced by legend and sorrow. The blue I had grown
to expect by the letterbox had one chance, and I seem to have
forgotten the nature of chance. I thought my faith was sufficient
but I was mistaken. Faith moves mountains, I have no doubt,
but only if mountains exist.

The long slow abdomens surface in the night

i.

and eat my basil, marigolds. The sheen of their silver trail
is the manna they leave, almost substance, proof
of their existence, hunger. I've read *they are deterred*
by basil, marigolds, but these ones pull my new shoots
into their slick bellies. I want to call them *invaders,*
but here I sit in a worker's cottage upside-down, an immigrant
planting cornflowers and poppies to remind me of home.
I want to say *the snail has no right to my seedlings*,
but we're the same: here by accident, thriving
at a cost we can't calculate. I went to the National Gallery
to appreciate my new walls. The Australian landscape
is painted with an honest brush. Lorraine Connelly-Northey
makes fabric out of sheet metal to explain white and black,
the intersection of boomerang and chain. *Woomera* is foreign
to me, so I go to Wikipedia and explore the complicated
history of my new country, an old country, a word—
I discover my snail is a metaphor for everything. It is time

ii.

for weapons. *The Green Gardener* tells me to crush
eggshells, sprinkle them around my basil so I can
slice my night creatures open. I'm drawing up my defense
strategy. Wikipedia tells me about *Fire in the Desert*, a village
populated by a people preoccupied with calculation, plotting
the trajectory of missiles in a cold war. *It was appropriate,*
someone writes, *for the village to be named after the woomera.*
I carry my eggshells to the garden in a small bowl, and launch
my weapons into my slight garden. Woomera, the territory,
is the size of England. It strikes me everything is the size of England:
Louisiana, tar sands in Fort McMurray, even this poem:
the only gravity I can calculate. My equation looks like this:
Woomera over snail = the velocity of Lorraine's possum. Is it stationary
or is it airborne before it reaches me? An artist slices
the tender belly open, throws what she has against the bare wall
of the gallery, vast and empty. Not because the desert
is fertile, but because someone has always lived there, because
someone has always been carving a long-range spear, testing
a throwing arm. I saw her cloak hanging on a white wall
and it pierced my heart. *It isn't me*, I wanted to say, but it was
my blood that spilled.

So the real question is, how necessary is a cornflower?

i.

The eggshells aren't working. Perhaps my night scalpel is
too late. Snails nibble their last supper and go home to bleed
or ooze or die — however it is they expire. *You should
get a blue-tongued lizard*, my friend tells me. I could
fasten a lizard to my fence so it can flick its tongue all night,
save my sprouts. Until now, I have wanted only to deter them,
but perhaps total annihilation is the only solution. I could
drown them in Heineken or something thicker: Guinness.
They'd prefer the darker brew, Greg says. For the first time
I contemplate poison, a pinch of copper, mustard gas, cyanide.
I won't wipe out all snails, just the ones in my cornflowers,
just the ones that take everything and leave me nothing.
My ethics are tired. I spent the evening flinging soggy projectiles
over my fence. This morning a boy on a trike flattened them,
satisfied by the sound. We are made for war

ii.

but it has to stop somewhere. The part of me
that aches for accord says *don't poison your well*
so I go online, read about nerve gas. A Nazarene
and an Indian pacifist twist into my vengeance—
it's inconvenient, the barometer at my core.
A nation can be judged by how it treats its animals,
I'm told before I exist. *The snail isn't from here*,
I plead with my secret Gandhi, but I'm in no position
to make claims. We both know I'm foreign too
and I'm still taking baths. *I could change*, I tell him,
plant something else: desert peas or succulents. He's dust
but he's still urging love against us, his words keep
reverberating on all the canyon walls: the grand ones
and the small chasm between my house and the fence,
the one the snails leak through. *I object to violence*, he said.
You know the rest:

                    (the way violence appears to do good,
the way that good is temporary, the way the evil it does is
permanent. If I go Roman and poison the watering hole,
I will have bent something, traded one small flower
for the future of a boy on a trike, the universe).

I'm told the telephone was an inevitability, and harnessing

fire, or at least learning how to tend flame. The wheel,
which was dormant awhile, waiting to roll us home
and afar. We've sought momentum since our first spark,
a way to twirl faster, dance harder. We spin our music,
dirty sweaters in our washing machines. We burn what burns
for speed: hydrogen and coal and even the mango curry
I ate last night with a cup of rice that will power me to noon.
We comprise a desire for ignition and we dreamed
the phoenix because it's not such a conundrum, ascendance
from ashes. Think of glass and Jack pine, even Pompeii
which strikes us as beautiful not because of sorrow
but because of what fire can preserve. We are explained
by Vesuvius and pottery shards, the Hindenburg
and Ford. We are two wheels and a pair of pedals
fuelled by the heat of my body, fruit and cumin
burning up my blue rivers. We are expressed by the friction
of a rooster on a hen, cheap Pyrex knock-offs exploding
in the microwave. I'm told our bodies are mostly water
but I tell you: our hearts are ablaze. We spend our lives
pouring our bodies into that muscle to put the flame out
so it can burn again, will-o'-the-wisp. I think we are
always putting out the same inferno, taming what cannot be
yoked, and can: the speed of a brush fire, a naked body
claiming another, me blasting on my bicycle — flammable
and quenched by love and rice and the state of fire,
the future.

This morning the neighbour woke me with music, her voice

i.

hurry up dearies to the magpies, yesterday's leftovers
shaking in a pan. From behind my blind I heard the lift
of wing from body, the weightlessness of winged weight
in that 7 a.m. blue as they dropped from gutter to pan.
They sang back to her without words, shook their bells,
strung chords of syllables, pleasure. These are the same
corvids that war in my garden, dive-bomb for possession
of candy wrappers, things that land without clanging.
There is a theory: *every sound continues to reverberate
after it is made.* In this way the world expands: it bursts
with the ringing of new bicycle chimes, the hush of wheat,
holy bells and forks scraping onions or lard, flipping
fish. A dry pitcher is full of the rush of water, the memory
of what it bore. Our mothers love us because they hear us
in our cribs demanding love and milk. I love exponentially
because I am flooding my house with noise, because
this room is clamouring, a symphony I'm not tuned to
but hear nonetheless. Our bedroom is night after night
of your feet on the floor, the bed against the wall. I wake
to hear the collective sigh of love after love, music upon
music, magpies and magpies. Of course —

ii.

there is more to the story. There always is. Our house is
the scrape of its foundations, trowel after trowel, grunts
of hungry men, fury, failure. I occupy the cacophony
of the dead, the history of what once stood on my path:
a lost child 2000 years ago, a marsupial tiger pawing
grass, tearing at the kneecap of a kangaroo, licking
her young, curled into a tuft. This house is broadcasting
September 1939, a girl over the handlebars at my window.
There is a couple in pyjamas whispering, worrying *why
did Julian do it, did we create him?* Is sound tethered
or does it stray? Do waves of grief cross oceans, slip in
front doors? Has Oma Heerema drifted from Holland
to peg clothes in my yard, hum Dutch hymns, kneel
at my bed and pray God to end the war? Julian began
his cascade at Leila's corner, surrendered at mine. So we
lie awake at night and listen to gunshot we cannot hear. Is this
why Leila sprayed her wall: *Love is the only reality?* We are
sound, inaudible ripples, fallen vases, every spoken language,
every splash in a pool, every knife dropped to the floor.
We are ululation, spoons on bars, horses on stone, lost
words, monkey bars, chaff. We are sheet music, a score
we can only read in the dark.

There is a theory that all the world is composed

of a single element. In presocratic times, we believed
every object was made of air or water. And today
we're still searching for singularity, sifting the smallest
objects we can imagine, quarks and antiquarks,
for our grammar. Einstein probed beneath a language
of particles, atoms, protons. It's not such a leap
to believe every object is a cocktail of the same
ingredients. Imagine we are all made of water
or desire, catalyzed by light. Imagine our shape
depends only on the slant of sun, how warm we are
when we begin to begin. The earth is a cell, I am
mass and electricity, friction and volume. We are
contained by a membrane. We are spinning, spun.
I don't know if we are flying to anything or away
from everything or if we are only twirling on the floor
with no trajectory. What I do know is that we are
justified by objects we can't understand: dogs dreaming,
a violin, an anglerfish in the dark. I don't comprehend
sienna, my new country, but somehow light passing
through suspended fabric, the shadow of a magpie
clarified this place, and at the same time me, spiralling
in Fitzroy North, explained by a window, composed
of what I do not know.

We used to believe a lot of things, and I still know

I could walk on water if I had enough faith. I'm trying to
believe in spontaneous generation, that it's possible to stride
to the end of the earth and leap, wings out, feet first and glide
into oblivion. I can imagine a tuft of lobelia shivering on the edge
of that bottomless chasm. I like the idea of Jupiter, Galilean moons
wheeling around me. The truth: I am at the centre of the universe
and so are you, though it's bizarre and impossible. We are
only as big as what we discern. This means despite the fact
that you can pinch yourself — *go on, do it* — I need faith to believe
you exist because I can't see you, because you haven't whispered
to me, scraped a chair across my studio, kissed me. Here's what I think:
we've disproved a lot of theories that are true. When I discovered
the tooth-fairy was my mother, nothing was dashed — I learned wings
are secrets. I discovered that my mother could fly. I've heard
we aren't made of earth, air, water, fire. And you believe that I exist
without proof (except this poem which is only an idea). Let me tell you
what I am made of. I am alizarin and charcoal, the part of you
that loves a red wheelbarrow. We are identical and opposite, we are
at the centre of a universe made with different ingredients. I know
men who are comprised of sea salt and the smell of bread. We are only
as big as our walls and we are burning because what we want to know
is the same as what we need to know.

                                              This is what will save us
in the end. I'll show you: picture my studio and the spider I tried to kill,
the one I whispered to before the cup came down. *Sorry,* I said, *I must
kill you because I am not sure.* In the end, I didn't. I didn't know
if it was poison. Uncertainty isn't adequate. Seems like nothing,
I know, but it is everything.

I've tried not to write a poem about roadkill for weeks

but my friend reminded me of Seamus Heaney's skunk, tail-up.
Write a poem about anything, she said, *if you need to.* You see,
in this heat I've been thinking of carcasses on county road 17.
I've been trying to recall their parabola. There are absences here:
no snow shovels leaning against brick in summer. Boxed in traffic
I don't contemplate *je me souviens* out of the blue. I suppose
there's not much difference between colliding with a deer
or a kangaroo. Both browsers have evolved their own syntax
for bounding, both lose everything when they hit a windshield.
Motorists here are advised to check the pouch of a crumpled doe
and I can't imagine the courage to open the envelope of her body,
search for a petrified survivor. My mom hit a deer in town,
I'm sorry, ma'am, the officer said, *you may want to turn your head*
as he pulled out his black handle and aimed for the head. Disaster
always comes out of nowhere, mid stride. What doesn't kill us
robs us of something: hope or mobility, immortality. The highway
is a metaphor for everything — the line between here and hereafter,
a kind of Styx, a ribbon between houses, dunes. When I was 8
I pedalled over a garter snake, was terrified by the prospect
that I could kill something
by not noticing it.

Confessions

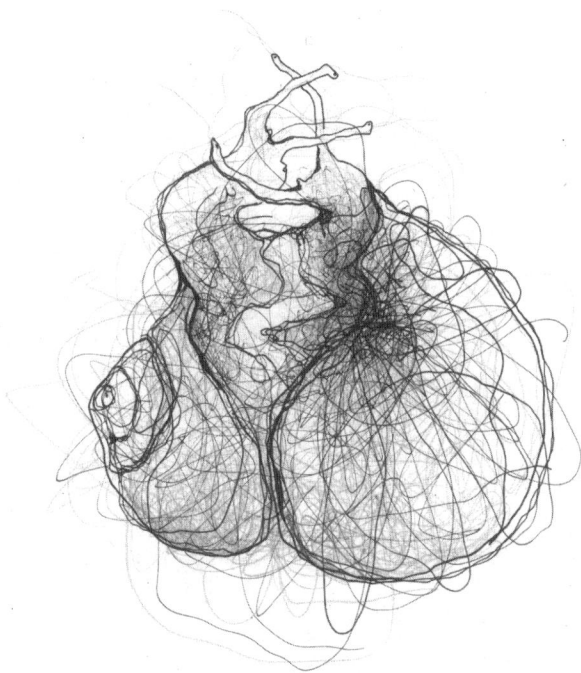

Confessions to My Sweetheart Regarding a Piece of Meat

i.

Just a nibble of the certainty of my expiry date

I don't usually do things behind your back, except
those red shoes when we were broke. I justified myself:
they'll bring me home to you. I was convinced I might
click three times home when I needed. And now this:
I've secreted a chunk of cow into our sofa. There's a reason —
I didn't get the chance to see Jana Sterbak's dress, the one
for the albino anorectic, and I want to smell it, touch it. I want
to watch it crisp and sink. I thought I might put the meat on
display, hang it in full sunlight, watch it rot. My proposal
was met with adjectives so I've had to compromise, meaning
I said I wouldn't do it, but I lied. I've cut a swath from Jana's
robes, from our *round steak family pack,* and I've hidden it
in a clear Tupperware. I confess, it's not my first vile act:
in grade 5 I filled 12 ice cream pails with *apple core, fried rice,*
milk, cucumber peels, pits. In the name of science I opened
each tub, asked my family to rate the odour. *Water and darkness*
smelled worst, I tell you, my fork in the steak that isn't in the sofa.
You know where I'm going, so you take a bite. *It's not the same*
as raw beef dangling off the side of our house, you say.
I don't know.

ii.

The container is not as sealed as I thought it was:

anyone who tells you Tupperware is airtight is lying.
Pandora's must have had a better seal, else all plagues
would have leaked out long before she got curious. My studio
is saturated with something sweet and terrible, white spots
on red flesh. My fabric scrap has soured. I thought I could
hide it from you, but sooner or later you'll smell death
in our house, look for the source, the fridge unplugged,
some closeted fortune establishing a new civilization
in the bottom drawer. Long ago our scientists had faith
that flies miraculously soar out of blade steaks. Humans
are always looking for miracles. We want to believe
that something can be drawn from nothing, that death
is fertile, that wings present themselves out of thin air.
I'm inclined myself: I grew up believing a sculptor
puffed into the nostrils of a clay man, twisted me from a rib.
I knew that human beings were created by God's bellows,
forged from loneliness and longing. It's not so hard to believe
that solitude is the catalyst for life. This steak is our substance.
It has the tang of the future, your grandma when her body began
to annex her mind. We all smell something different when we
catch a whiff of fate. For your grandma: finally a deep sleep
and for the long eel, a banquet. For us all, the container
can't stifle the odour of the future. Death is the evidence we need
to reconcile the miracle of existing, growing sweet and weak,
ending like we began.

iii.

Danse macabre, a small jig for a Tupperware

Well, I've banished the box to the outdoors. I've tucked it
behind the gazanias and a big grey stone. It will take some time
for the meat to steep, for the neighbours to notice the stench.
In '89 my family drove past a decomposing calf in the ditch
for a month before we knew it was there, before we had to
roll up the windows, plug our noses, zoom faster. I investigated
alone on my banana seat bicycle. I needed to figure out
the curve of decay, the way we hollow, drop. I wanted to look
at its hooves, savour fear. I didn't have the words then for mortality,
temporality, but I needed to honour what I couldn't understand.
I heaved a stone onto its body, a marker so I could remember it
when it had vanished. My container will be discovered
by a joyful dog, but until then I am witnessing the edges losing
definition, the meat receding. I see its dimming blush, my own
transience. My granddaddy had ears like a frisbee cut in half—
Old people's ears don't grow, he said, *parts of our bodies become*
less important as we fade. I want to wear Jana's dress, boogie
in it before it gets stiff. I want to think about your grandma's
hands, bones. I want to contemplate her knees, the way her throat
got too tight for her voice, how her exasperation with your mom
receded, made way for music, finger-tapping. As we exit,
those of us who have a scrap of sense learn to dance.

iv.

Jana's flank was cured, mine is a plague.

In fact, I'm nervous about opening the box. In the heat
there's been condensation, but I can still see the fortune
that awaits the fool who opens it. The meat is gone, replaced
by fat grubs that have generated spontaneously, wriggled
into existence in my makeshift greenhouse. I've begun
to contemplate ugliness, vanity. I want to know how to age
gracefully, how to love my body without letting it die too early,
too late. I'm curious whether anything can be cured, preserved.
A part of me believes in letting the ground lie fallow, silence
after fisticuffs with you instead of heat and limbs, apology.
A fraction of me refuses doctors, rumbles around the house
in the cotton I slept in. Should we live like we're going to die,
and what does that mean? Should I aspire to be a container
for recklessness and prudence? Jana says I should
sew up, trim up, make impossible dresses and love what is
destined for dirt. I should hide what matters in secret places:
the cave of your ear. I suppose I am charged to find beauty
in odd places, old places, boxes and bones. I'm not choosing
between disparate things. I am only deciding to dance
or not to dance.

Eadweard Muybridge captured motion by making it still

and so I am painting rain on my parents' roof. Some things
cannot be silenced. A running horse is never still, rain
is always landing. My parents were always moving away
from each other. What, exactly, do we do when we paint?
Are we cartographers of memory, are we painting ourselves
freeze frame, documenting what we wanted, one thought
so still it is impossible? Lately I have been wondering
what we lose when the people we love stop loving
each other.

My parents, when they shared a tin roof,
borrowed an underwater love story from another couple:
The Abyss. They divorced and we didn't know who to return it to.
This painting is a map of a place I once knew, my bed
on the other side of my parents' wall, the still of night, rain.
Time, whatever you believe, has momentum. A captive moment
does not exist. There is no motion in stasis or rain unlanded.
A painting is a portrait of the impossible, a past in stasis
hanging on a wall. I began this, language hung on a page,
in the present which has already moved on. It doesn't matter
if you think time is wheel or a line, or a human construct.
It doesn't matter if the horse, for a split second, is airborne.
What matters is that when you ride a horse you feel weightless,
when it rains something inside you spins, when you paint you find
the centre of something, as simple as falling asleep
to the sound of rain, your father talking to your mother, shoes
dropping on the floor, change spilling onto the dresser, voices
in the dark.

An Apologetic to Cockroaches from the Future

i.

This is what I'm stuffing into a bottle, to bury in our Mesozoic
so that one day when we have become the dinosaurs
cockroaches, evolved and resilient, will have pity on us,
the circumstances of our deluge, the inevitable
extinction of *homo sapiens*, a word that falls so short
of what we are capable of. Perhaps, dear cockroaches,
you'll forgive us, come to believe something necessary
and particular washed out when we did. I want the future
to deliver the verdict, but the future is opaque. My apologetic
is this: there's a small boy I love. I don't know why
there's no equation for the puzzle of the heart. I love him
because I imagine him growing, in green flip-flops, reading
Christopher Paolini at a bus stop. I love him because

ii.

today he was bitten by a spider and almost faded. He was
translucent, and when the colour shivered from him, I felt
pity for us all. The future is terrible and complicated
and, even though we've earned our destiny, I'd like to think
a child can vindicate us. He proves how close to holiness we are
when we are frightened. I bicycled home after, closed my eyes
to feel the hill, the warm slide of eucalyptus over my body.
When I opened them there was a headless dove on the asphalt,
a strewn body, evidence that we are collision and compassion.
Our first art was fingerprints on stone and we haven't left that cave.
That's why I'm tapping keys, pressing my hands on a white page,
the walls, perplexed and enamoured by the accident of substance.
Gabosale makes baskets so I can carry what matters; Mosophane
peels an orange to teach me a new language; Gerald scatters grain
for failing birds. It's not what we are that makes us. It's how
we fade. It's the fact that we haven't figured out what we're doing
here, or how to be here. But we crave a brush with meaning.
We are, as it turns out, a spider bite: a blemish
of infinite potential.

Finish with your signature
silently in the corner. You can
remember what you wanted,
something beautiful, something ———

Notes

"Eadweard Muybridge captured motion by making it still," *Branch Magazine*, Volume 2.2, 2010.

"Eating quince with musicians," *Descant*, Summer Issue, 2010 (D149).

"Confessions to my sweetheart regarding a piece of meat," *Dandelion Magazine*, Volume 35.2, 2010.

The section *Anatomy for the Artist* was first published as a chapbook by Greenboathouse Press in 2009.

"Getting out of the house," *Carousel Magazine*, Issue 23, 2008.

"Prescriptions for Katherine (not your real name)," *Carousel Magazine*, Issue 23, 2008.

"How to cut a chicken into little pieces," *Carousel Magazine*, Issue 23, 2008.

"Anatomy for the artist," *The Malahat Review*, Issue 163, 2008.

"The starting point of any description of human anatomy," *The Malahat Review*, Issue 163, 2008.

"Georgia, I'm sorry you're dead," *The Antigonish Review*, Issue 154, 2008.

"Georgia's recipes, somehow," *The Antigonish Review*, Issue 154, 2008.

"Georgia's pelvis III and IV," *The Antigonish Review*, Issue 154, 2008.

Excerpts from Gerald, God and the Chickens was first published as a chapbook by Frog Hollow Press in 2008.

Acknowledgements

Thanks Deborah, Kurt, Annika, and Isabella for sharing your home while many of these poems were being written. For others who gave me a roof in Australia: Ruth and Joel, Simon and Judy, and James — thank you.

Katherine, I hope someday the right person catches you when you fall. DF, I hope someday the doctors tell you what's right with you. Gerald, I hope one day you can read poems again.

Thanks Mom, for giving me courage and crayons. Thanks Rachel and Joshua, for being you. Thanks Oma, for singing. Thanks Opa, for reading. Thanks Dad, for unwavering adoration. Lisa, thank you for your golden mallet, your golden friendship — for two crows joy. Thanks Erin, for your horse latitudes and other sweet fuels. Thanks Leila, for spray-painting love on your wall. Thanks Olga, for your turquoise encouragement. Thanks Gabosale, for teaching me more than how to make a basket. Thanks Mosophane, for the brief moment our lives intersected. Caroline, thank you for your lenses. Thanks Nan, for ineffable friendship. Laura, I wouldn't write if I didn't have you to write to.

Thanks Vanessa at Goose Lane, for your light touch.

Thanks Amy, Bryan, Cat, Chris, Christina, Dean, Denise, Dionne, Eleni, Fred, Gigi, Jonathan, Lisa A., Queenie, Sasha, Shauna, Simon C., Thomas, Teema, and Wesley. Maya Angelou is quoted as saying: "I've learned that people will forget what you said, people will forget what you did, but people will never forget how you made them feel" — thank you for how you make me feel. If you didn't make me feel, I wouldn't have anything to say. And I like saying.

photo: Caroline Andrews

Jessica Hiemstra-van der Horst is an artist and writer. Her poems have appeared in *Descant*, *Room*, *Arc*, and *The Malahat Review*, and in anthologies such as *Approaches to Poetry: the pre-poem moment*.